FLEABAG SHRINE

DIVERSE PARTICULARS
APROPOS OF
NO. 9 RUE GÎT-LE-COEUR

FLEABAG SHRINE:
Diverse Particulars Apropos of
No. 9 rue Gît-le-Coeur

GREGORY STEPHENSON

Ober-Limbo Verlag

Published by Ober-Limbo Verlag
Heidelberg, Germany

ISBN 978-87-971569-3-3

Cover design, layout & translations from the French
by Birgit Stephenson

For Birgit

My Brilliant Friend

RUE GIT-LE-CŒUR

FLEABAG SHRINE:
Diverse Particulars Apropos of
No. 9 rue Gît-le-Coeur

*"the beat hotel, a fleabag shrine in a section of Paris
where passersby move out of the way for rats."*
Time Magazine November 30, 1962

"rue Gît-le-Coeur, au nom symbolique évident."
Gilles Dorion

A fortunate convergence of persons and circumstances, a fertile,
fugitive interlude in the cultural flux: the late 1950s and early
1960s in a nameless old hotel at no. 9 rue Gît-le-Coeur on the left
bank of the river Seine in Paris. Aspiring poets, writers, painters,
actors, photographers, musicians and others are drawn together
there to live frugally under the same ancient gray slate roof. For a
heady spell the old hotel becomes a forward operating base of
imaginative expression. Then, abruptly the hotel is sold and is
closed for remodelling. The residents disperse to their several
fates. "It scatters and it gathers," Heraclitus writes, "it comes and
it goes." *Here lies the heart,* indeed.

The somewhat random bits of information heaped
hereinbelow are humbly intended as explanatory notes of an
oblique kind, subsidiary to (and presupposing a familiarity with)
two fine books bearing the same title and treating the same

subject: Harold Chapman's impressive photographic record, *The Beat Hotel* (1984) and Barry Miles' admirable chronicle, *The Beat Hotel: Ginsberg, Burroughs and Corso in Paris, 1957-1963* (2000.) My aim is merely to supplement by a little the facts and backgrounds concerning the hotel and its environs provided in those two books, strictly avoiding any repetition of sources used or information presented by their authors. In the absence of an ardent acquaintance on the part of the reader with the above-named books by Harold Chapman and Barry Miles, these notes must necessarily be of very meagre interest, indeed.

According to information kindly provided to me by Monsieur Francois Gasnault of the Archives de Paris, the building at no. 9 rue Gît-le-Coeur was transformed into a hotel during the 1870s. The "Cadastre de 1876," an official survey of property undertaken by the city of Paris, gives the name of the building at that time as Hotel de Montpellier and describes the rooms within as furnished. In a photograph taken of the rue Gît-le-Coeur (looking in the direction of the rue Saint André des Arts) during the Paris flood of January 1910, there appear to be three hotels on the east side of the street between the Quai des Grands Augustins and the rue de l'Hirondelle. (See Appendix I, page 45.) I am somewhat uncertain as to which of these was later to become the fabled Beat Hotel, but I believe it to be the second (middle) one of the three depicted on the left of the photo. I conclude this because the position on the street seems right and because a drain pipe is visible, standing a bit beyond the adjacent surface of the facade just to the north of the building, and additionally, there is a sign affixed to the front of the mid-positioned hotel advertising *Vins, Liquers* and something else not clear enough to be read which indicates the presence there of a café, as, indeed, there was still during the time that the Monsieur and Madame Rachou operated the hotel. (Visible in Harold Chapman's photos, a hand-lettered, painted sign above the doors of the Beat Hotel reads: VINS CAFÉ LIQUERS.)

Worthy of notice in terms of the perennially raffish character of the rue Gît-le-Coeur is the presence there in 1795 of a printer called Jean-Nicolas Barba who was "a notorious literary pirate and dealer in pornography," publishing illegal editions of the Marquis de Sade's *Justine*. (*Publishing and Cultural Politics in Revolutionary Paris, 1789-1810* by Carla Hesse, University of California Press, 1991, p. 199.) During the heyday of the Beat Hotel (ca. 1957 to 1963) the building at no. 5 rue Gît-le-Coeur was occupied by another pornographic printer-publisher, Bronislaw Kaminsky, aka "Bruno Durocher," who during the late 1950s and early 1960s published English-language pornographic novels under the imprints of the Mediterranean Press, the Pall Mall Press and Week End Books. According to Patrick Kearney, author of *A Checklist of the Paris Competitors of the Olympia Press*, Kaminsky was a minor poet who had once enjoyed a reputation as "the Polish Rimbaud," after the publication of his first volume of poetry at the age of seventeen. Kearney further recounts that Kaminsky "spent the war years in concentration camps and settled in Paris in 1945." (Scissors & Paste Bibliographies, Santa Rosa, Ca: 2019, p. 16.)

By way of contrast to these dubious enterprises and with respect to the mystical and occult inclinations of certain of the Beat Hotel's residents, it is of interest to note that the silent Indian mystic Meher Baba (1894-1969) who claimed to be an Avatar or God in human form, lived for a time in 1936 as a guest of Consuelo and Alfredo Sides in their apartment at no.1 rue Gît-le-Coeur. Disparate psychic influences may thus be seen to have contended and mingled on this short and narrow street.

The somewhat sinister and unsavoury reputation attached to the rue Gît-le-Coeur in the Paris of the 19th century is drawn upon in *Idols, or The Secret of the rue Chausée d'Antin,* by French novelist Raoul de Navery (nom-de-plume of Madame Marie-Eugene Saffray 1829-1885.) The narrative (the original French title of which I have been unable to ascertain) takes place soon after the renovation of Paris undertaken by Georges-Eugène Haussman and is centered in part upon a group of thieves – the Knights of the Black Cap – and their chieftain and fence, Father Methuselah, whose dodgy shop with its secret cellar is located on the rue Gît-le-Coeur: *"In the very heart of Paris, near the quays and bordering upon the river, in the broad light of day and in a pleasant neighbourhood is a street or rather a narrow lane, through the center of which runs a muddy stream and where high dark walls shut out the rays of the sun. The rue Gît-le-Coeur, one of the oldest streets in that ancient Paris which has disappeared under the progress of modern improvements, remained what it was in the middle ages. But little more and it would require to have an iron chain stretched at either extremity of it, which together with the watch might enable honest citizens of Paris to sleep in peace.*

About half way down this street, some four years before this story opens, stood a squalid shop, full of rubbish, rusty iron, broken or mended china, old clothes, curtains ready to fall into dust, instruments of all trades which men may lawfully and openly pursue. We say lawfully and openly, for in dark corners of the shop were huge bunches of keys of every conceivable form, finely pointed chisels, files of exquisite perfection, pincers that were masterpieces in their kind, in fine, a whole collection of disavowed articles or articles which were seldom called for in any other language than slang. (Idols, or, The Secret of the rue Chausée d'Antin, New York: Benzinger Brothers, 1882.)

A depiction of the rue Gît-le-Coeur as it impressed a foreign observer during the last quarter of the 19th century is to be found in a little-known novel titled *Under the Red Flag* (London & New York: 1883) written by M.E. Barrett. (Mary Elizabeth Barrett, 1835-1915.) The novel is set during the Paris Commune and concerns the fate of two orphaned Irish girls living in France whose desperate poverty compels them to take lodging in furnished rooms on the rue Gît-le-Coeur. Of the street, Barrett writes: *"The Rue Gît le Coeur is not one of the fashionable streets of Paris. ... Beauty and fashion never visit the spot. It has hardly any place on the map of Paris. ... Gît le Coeur is a narrow shabby little street, hidden somewhere in the densely populated district between the Boulevard St. Michel and the Rue des Saints Peres ... far from the haunts of pleasure, from the famous restaurants, from clubs and cafés, from parks and parterres, from opera-house and aristocratic hotel. It is a narrow street – crooked too – and the houses are of the shabbiest."* The rooms hired by the two girls are described as *"very small, very shabby"* but there is to be found, they are told, *"nothing so cheap in all Paris."* (Citations from the Tauchnitz edition, Hamburg: 1884, pp. 20-21, 54.)

Written nearly two decades later than Barrett's novel, a passage in *Monsieur Bergeret à Paris* by Anatole France (Paris: C. Lévy, 1901) conveys both the ancient charm and the sordidness of the rue Gît-le-Coeur around the year 1900, as perceived by the eponymous protagonist: *"Meanwhile, he continued to go house-hunting, but taking an imaginative approach. Old houses pleased him because their stones seemed to address him. The rue Gît-le-Cœur held a particular attraction for him, and whenever he saw a notice announcing an apartment for rent, beside the keystone of a gateway or on a door which had once been flanked by a wrought-iron rail, he would mount the stairs, accompanied by a squalid concierge. They would enter into an atmosphere reeking of countless generations of rats, a fug which was amplified from floor to floor by the emanation of cooking from destitute kitchens. The workshops of bookbinders or box-makers at times added to the air an awful stench of rotten glue. And Monsieur Bergeret would go on his way filled with sadness and discouragement."* (p. 34.)

A somewhat more detailed depiction of the street and its ambience two decades further on – during the 1920s – occurs in another obscure English-language novel, *The Black Gale* by Samuel Shellabarger (New York: The Century Company, 1929.) In this novel, the rue Gît-le-Coeur represents the lowest level of poverty, vice and degradation, the nadir of hope, a dark underworld inhabited by the broken, the cunning and the greedy. Yet for the novel's hero and heroine, the street also becomes a locus of redemption. The novel traces the downfall of Morier Ravenel, a former aviator and war hero, a scholar and a professional gambler. Tall, graceful, prosperous, insouciant and honourable at the outset of the novel, his fortunes decline steadily and then precipitously, as does also his health. Impoverished and partially paralyzed, he ends in a wretched room in a hotel on the rue Gît-le-Coeur. There, after long searching, he is found by Jacklin, the woman who loves him and who now devotes all her energies to gladdening and enhancing his miserable life. She lives with him there in his seedy, reeky hotel and to his squalid room brings flowers and pictures to brighten the shabby walls. In this way, both lovers regain will and belief. In the end, the street is seen as having rendered both of them a service: *"It had been a bitter antidote to the insubstantial earlier dreaming; it had presented crude actuality, and had shown the vast distress of the world underlying its rare festivals."* Clearly, in this regard, the author employs the name of the street as suggestive of the salvatory power of the heart's affections.

The novel's description of the street and the hotel presents a unique picture of the rue Gît-le-Coeur only a few decades before the advent of the hotel as a Beat outpost: *"The rue Gît-le-Coeur is one of that network of streets, scrambled at haphazard, narrow and malodorous ... Its chief claim to interest is antiquity, picturesque shabbiness, and reminiscences of the past – that is if the visitor is curious and sympathetic. Otherwise, he will find himself simply in a maze of passages, weather-rotted and damp, that teem with life, human and parasitic. On the sanitary chart of Paris, this quarter is stained black; and black it is in those courts, where the sun has never slanted beneath the roof-gutters, and of which the stones drip moisture that recalls the sweat of disease. Here the air is stagnant and cold. It is the breath of tuberculosis, poverty, and dirt. ... Its prevailing smell, which clings acidly to everything, is a blending of foul clothes, garbage, and ordure."*

The "hotel meublé" (furnished rooms) where Ravenel lodges and where Jacklin finds him is described in the following manner: *"Inside, it was colder than without, a rancid, stagnant cold that recalled a vegetable cellar ... And it was darker ... The Staircase was narrow and the banister, crazy with age, trembled beneath her hand as she groped upward through almost complete darkness, until at length a gray semblance of light from an inside window marked the landing. There followed an expanse of uncarpeted hall and broken plaster; then another dim shaft of steps ... a second expanse of blistered plaster, broken by nondescript doors."* Ravenel's lodging on the second floor is *"a small, bare room, lighted only from the court ... there was a bed, a table, a chair and then another chair near the window."* This portrayal of a nameless hotel on the rue Gît-le-Coeur by Samuel Shellabarger will be seen to correspond in several particulars both to the earlier depictions by M.E. Barrett and Anatole France and to later descriptions written by some of the bohemian residents of the Beat Hotel, which was – it will be recalled – a "class 13" establishment, that is one meeting only the barest minimum of standards of health and safety as prescribed under French law.

It is curious to consider that the cramped and unwholesome rookeries of the rue Gît-le-Coeur occupied by wretched generations of the Paris poor, and later by impecunious students and bohemians, were once part of palatial, richly appointed and ornate apartments belonging to nobility. (*A Travers le Quartier Latin* by Octave Charpantier, Paris: Editions D'Art, 1924, p. 16.) And, of course, it is equally curious to consider that the dilapidated, primitive premises of the Beat Hotel were subsequently to be transformed into the sumptuous four star Relais Hotel du Vieux Paris that is currently situated within the very structure of the former "fleabag shrine."

In their account of the liberation of Paris occurring on August 25, 1944, authors Larry Collins and Dominique Lapierre recount the following incident – a scene as horrific as any in William Burroughs' *Naked Lunch* – taking place during fighting on the Left Bank between the FFI (French Forces of the Interior) and soldiers of the German Wehrmacht: *"In the tangle of twisting alleys between the Seine and Saint-Germain-des-Prés, on streets with names as quaint as the rue du Chats-qui-Pêche and rue Gît-le-Coeur, hidden FFI squads trapped four truckloads of German soldiers. Some of them, their uniforms blazing from the splatterings of Molotov cocktails, ran screaming through scenic little sides streets, human torches in a thousand-year-old haven of human amusement."* (*Is Paris Burning?* New York: Simon & Schuster, p. 149.)

Allusions to the rue Gît-le-Coeur are made in a number of literary works. In James Joyce's *Ulysses* (1922) the former wife of Irish exile Kevin Egan, an acquaintance of Stephen Dedalus during his sojourns in Paris, is said to be living *"quite nicey comfy without her outcast man, madame in rue Gît-le-Coeur, canary and two buck lodgers."* (*Ulysses* by James Joyce, New York: Random House, 1946, p.44.) The street also makes an appearance in an automatic poem titled "Tournesol" (Sunflower) transcribed by André Breton in 1923, describing a walk taken by a young woman through the night streets of Paris from Les Halles to the rue Gît-le-Coeur. *"Rue Gît-le-Coeur les timbres n'étaient plus les memes,"* (Rue Gît-le-Coeur resonances no longer rang the same) reads one enigmatic line. Breton was later to discover that the poem was uncannily prophetic of his fateful amorous encounter eleven years later with the painter Jacqueline Lamba with whom on the night of their meeting he walked from Pigalle to the rue Gît-le-Coeur, inadvertently (or unconsciously) following much of the same route and passing the same landmarks as set forth in "Tournesol." (*André Breton: Le Grand Indésirable* by Henri Béhar, Paris: Fayard, 2005, p. 311.)

The Czech poet Vitezslav Nezval (1900-1958) – co-founder of the Czech Surrealist movement – wrote a book of poetic essays titled *Ulice Gît-le-Coeur* (Rue Gît-le-Coeur) recounting vivid, enchanted moments from his stay in Paris in 1935, including cherished memories of a café on Gît-le-Coeur in which he met with his friends. (Prague: Frantisek Borovy, 1936.) Might this café have been the one operated by Madame Rachou on the ground floor of no. 9 rue-Git-le-Coeur? In 1941, while living in the United States in exile from German-occupied France, the celebrated French poet Saint-John Perse composed a poem titled "Poème à l'étrangère," (Poem to a Foreign Lady) in which the following words occur as a refrain: "Rue Gît-le-Coeur ... Rue Gît-le-Coeur ... chante tout bas l'Alienne sous ses lampes et ce sont là méprises de sa langue d'Étrangère." (Rue Gît-le-Coeur ... Rue Gît-le-Coeur ... sings the alien in a low voice beneath the street lamps, and such is the disdain of her foreign tongue.) A Swiss poet, Simone Cuendet, also inspired by the poetic name of the street, wrote a volume of poems entitled *Rue Gît-le-Coeur* (Lausanne: Les Terreaux, 1954.) Another collection of poems using a similar title is Arnolde de Kerchove's *Gît-le-Coeur: Poèmes 1957-1959* (Paris: Debresse, 1959.) There is a detective novel by Claude Valmont (nom-de-plume of Fernande Salzedo about whom no further information was to be found apart from a derisory description of her as a "bourgeoise désargentée" or a penniless former member of the middle class) with the intriguing title: *Le Drame de la rue Gît-le-Coeur* (Paris: Tallandier, 1933.)

Allusions to the rue Gît-le-Coeur also occur in French popular song. In 1955, Germaine Montero recorded a song titled "Rue Gît-le-Coeur," in which the narrator-singer addresses a prostitute named Lorraine whose regular round is Gît-le-Coeur. In the brief drama depicted in the song text Lorraine walks this "crooked street" waiting for customers to arrive, feeling increasingly uneasy that they have not yet come. Meanwhile, she must evade the police, who according to their mood, may arrest her or even strike her. Only the street itself pities her: "the stones are moved to see you so naked." (*Refrains de Paris*. Pathé EG 141m 45 rpm, lyrics by Luc Poret, music by Jacques Solet.) Another French song linking a prostitute with the rue Gît-le-Coeur is Juliette Greco's "Chambre 33" (room 33.) The lyric gives voice to a proudly independent prostitute who lives in a hotel room on the rue Gît-le-Coeur. She prefers, she says, to live alone "without a dog, without a husband, without a cat, without a pimp, in room 33, on the 3rd floor, rue Gît-le-Coeur." (*À L'Olympia,* Philips P70342L, 1966, LP.) A reference to the rue Gît-le-Coeur is also to be found in a song written and recorded by Francoise Hardy, "J'ai le Coeur Vide Aujourd'hui" (My heart is empty today) in which a first-person narrator recalls tender moments with a lover from whom she is now separated: "C'est drôle sans toi le Quai aux Fleurs / C'est drôle la vieille rue Gît-le-Coeur / Ces noms que j'amais tant ce soir me font pleurer." (It's strange without you at the flower marked / It's strange in the old rue Gît-le-Coeur / those names I dearly loved make me cry tonight.)

A collection of love poems written by Lord Lymington (Gerard Vernon Wallop 1898-1984) is titled *Gît-le-Coeur* (Paris: Black Sun Press, 1928) and there is a novel by Ludwig Bemelmans (1898-1962) called *The Street where the Heart Lies* (New York: The World Publishing Co. 1963.) I have skimmed the latter, but could find in it no description of the street to which the book's title refers. Both Lymington and Bemelmans once occupied premises at no. 1 rue Gît-le-Coeur, an elegant, upscale property with a view of the Seine, situated on the northeast corner of the Quai des Grands Augustins and the rue Gît-le-Coeur.

Apart from poems written by residents of the Beat Hotel (to which I will turn in due course) other poems inspired by the street have appeared in print. These include John Logan's "The Bridge of Change," which details a walk through Paris by the poet-speaker conveying in verse his reflections on events in the history of the city and ending with the lines: "I turn right, wandering a bit, and suddenly as if by chance, find myself on *this* street, and here I will wait, for it is our street, *Rue Gît-le-Coeur: Here Lies the Heart.*" (Title poem of *The Bridge of Change* Brockport: Boa Editions, 1978.) Two other poems by two other poets invoke the rue Gît-le-Coeur in their titles, and the first-person speakers of both poems would seem to be situated somewhere in that street as they compose the verses recording their reflections there, but in neither of the two poems is any further reference made to the street itself. "Midnight, Rue Gît-le-Coeur" by Maurice English is a prayer to God for deliverance of the speaker from the tormenting contrarieties of flesh and spirit, and for redemption of the world from violence and suffering. (The Sewanee Review, vol. 72, no. 2, Spring 1964.) "On the Rue Gît-le-Coeur: Mirage no. 9" by Michael Collins is a poem addressed by the speaker to a distant former lover living in the United States. A lament for lost love, the poem also contains an element of implied social criticism. (Callaloo, vol. 16, no. 2, Spring 1993.) In all three of these poems it is clear that the name of the street functions symbolically.

A clear allusion to the Beat Hotel and to the grand literary ideals – a belief in the revolutionary, redemptive power of poetry – held by certain poets (notably Allen Ginsberg and Gregory Corso) resident there occurs in Lawrence Felinghetti's lyrical novel, *Her* (1960) set in Paris during the postwar period: "*a wailing wild ragged band of American poets from the Rue Gît-le-Coeur rushed out of a side street into the middle of the boulevard ... singing and shouting that the Poetry Police were coming to save them, the Poetry Police were coming to save them all from death, Captain Poetry was coming to save the world from itself, to make the world safe for beauty and love, the Poetry Police had arrived to clean up the mass mess ...shouting wiggy formulas for eternal mad salvation, the Poetry Police were about to capture all libraries, newspapers, printing presses and automats and force their proprietors at pen's point to print nothing henceforth but headlines of pure poetry and menus of pure love... .*" (New York: New Directions, 1960, pp. 42-43. The same passage appears in

Ferlinghetti's second novel, *Love in the Days of Rage,* New York: E.P. Dutton, 1988.)

 Although the Beat Hotel gave refuge for a time to what must be seen as a unique concentration of expatriate poets, photographers, musicians, writers and painters all gathered at the same location, the young (and older) bohemian residents there were, in fact, part of a larger wave of a postwar migration of Americans and Britons to Paris, motivated in large measure by a then prevalent romantic image of the City of Light, not least perhaps the city's association with fashionable existentialism. In *Left Bank, Right Bank,* Joseph A. Barry's account of postwar Paris, the author states that by 1951 there were already 12,000 Americans living in Paris, their numbers divided neatly between the Right Bank and the Left Bank. (New York: W.W. Norton, 1951, p. 31.) Paris still enjoyed during this era considerable cachet as a kind of global capital of the arts, as well as of fashion and philosophy. Many aspiring young writers and artists were attracted to the city by the lingering glamour of the expatriate 1920s and 1930s, the mythic Modernist Paris of Ezra Pound, Gertrude Stein, James Joyce, Ernest Hemingway, F. Scott Fitzgerald and later Henry Miller, or by the presence there of celebrated, innovative artists, numerous small galleries and famous art schools such as the Académie de la Grande Chaumière and the École des Beaux Arts.

 Living in voluntary poverty, pursuing writing or painting or some other form of creative expression while living in a cheap, rundown hotel, availing oneself liberally of the drugs readily available in Paris, engaging in transient sexual relationships (and/or inter-racial or homosexual relationships), having a salacious novel published in the Traveller's Companion Series of the infamous Olympia Press – all of these were already by the late 1950s established traditions among the expatriate bohemian community resident in the Paris. In this sense, the residents of the Beat Hotel may be seen as a contingent and a continuation of the subcultural enclave (consisting of diverse coteries) situated since the end of World War II principally in the 5th and 6th arrondissements of the city of Paris. (That enclave itself a continuation of the experimentalism in the arts centered in Paris during the interwar years.)

Literary experimentation and innovation were thus a tradition among striving young expatriate writers in postwar Paris (carrying on the spirit of Joyce, Stein and Miller.) A number of English-language literary magazines (some short-lived) receptive to transgressive, culturally-subversive, cutting-edge writing had since the end of the war been edited and published in Paris. These included: *Points, Zero, Merlin, New Story, Locus Solus, Two Cities* and *The Paris Review*. A one-shot magazine called *Left Bank This Month* (Summer 1959) promoted work by several habitués of the Beat Hotel, including photographs of Harold Chapman, poetry by Gregory Corso and Kenneth Thomas Tindall, and a prose piece on the Beat Hotel (of which more immediately herebelow) written by hotel resident Verta Kali Smith. From 1961 to 1963, a newly started literary journal called *Olympia* also published writing by a number of residents of the Beat Hotel, including William Burroughs, Gregory Corso, Brion Gysin, Jonathan Kozol and Kay Johnson.

The earliest mention in print of "the Beat Hotel" under that designation would seem to be Verta Kali Smith's article (illustrated with photographs by Harold Chapman) in the above-named magazine, *Left Bank This Month*, edited by Ronald Sheridan. Ms. Smith's piece is of significance and interest both for her description of the street itself and of circumstances within the hotel: *"Among laundries, Chinese restaurants, frame makers and an African Oasis club lies number nine, otherwise known as the Beat*

Hotel, most exclusive hotel in Paris. Impossible to get into unless you know the key people, say the right things, carry a canvas under your arm or have long hair. ... The electricity is primitive ... the maximum load for each room is 40 watts. ... One can jump from

Oriental luxury to stark modern merely by climbing from the third to the fourth floor. The first floor is inhabited among others by a trumpeter who plays all night in the Moulin Rouge and practices all day in his room, a tuba playing painter, an American guitarist who

lives with her Greek lover, a crazy genius photographer and finally La Patronne."

Another article on the hotel, its tenants and its *patronne,* written by hotel resident Dixie Nimmo, appeared in *Town Magazine* (December 1962, pp. 92-95, 96.) Titled "The Dream Palace," the piece is illustrated with photos by "Duffy" (Brian Duffy) and consists of biographical sketches of and brief interviews with a half-dozen of the hotel residents, including William Burroughs, Kay Johnson, Harold Norse, John Howley, Brion Gysin and Ian Somerville.

The article presents a nuanced but predominantly favourable account of the experiences and opinions of the hotel's guests. William Burroughs holds forth upon the fold-in method and the relation between art and science. He states that he lives at 9 rue Gît-le-Coeur as "*a matter of convenience and economy. The hotel is cheap and relatively quiet with a perfect landlady. My publisher, Mr. Girodias of Olympia Press is located around the corner.* (p. 96.) " Kay Johnson expresses disappointment and a sense of isolation: "*I came here to find artistic friendship and found only loneliness. It was as if I were out in the Sahara desert.*" (p. 94.) John Howley is somewhat ambivalent: "*Paris has me hooked. She has an electric quality full of creative peril. But the complicated French mind gives me the impression that they still live underground, a vestige of the Occupation.*" (p. 95.)

Harold Norse is more sanguine about circumstances in Paris and among the young Beats at the hotel: "*In spite of Americanisation all over, Europe continues to have a relaxing effect which affords the body a chance to pursue individual aims and pursuits, especially in writing and painting that are not regarded as loafing and a waste of time or downright insanity. Henry Miller is the grand-daddy of us all. The least pornographic and the most natural man of our day. His influence has directly produced the Beat progeny, a social and spiritual revolution."* (pp. 94-95.)

The article concludes with an expression of admiration for the indefatigable *"blue-haired, pugnacious, kindly"* Madame Rachou, who acts as a watchdog for her clientele and is understanding when rent falls behind. She rises every morning at six *"opens the café doors at nine, keeps them open as late as residents and after-dinner visitors require. At the first hint of spring she moves tables out onto the pavement to catch the watery shafts of early sunlight, the air and gossip from the quays."* (p. 96.)

There is a clear disparity between the laudatory pieces on the Beat Hotel written by Verta Kali Smith and Dixie Nimmo and an article (like Ms. Smith's also illustrated with photographs by Harold Chapman) by "Yvette Alouette" appearing in the November 1964 issue of *Sir* magazine. Although the article is titled "The Amazing Beat Hotel," the tone of the text is consistently rude and mean-spirited – sneering, smirking, smart-assed and clearly written by a male American boor. (The author makes reference to G.I. slang for Turkish toilets, an expression not likely to have been in the lexicon of a young French woman.) The author establishes the scornfully abusive tone of the article at the outset by referring to the residents of the Beat Hotel as a *"motley crew of weirdies and wayout characters that infests number 9."* (*Infests,* mind you.) He (I'm certain the author is a male) confuses Allen Ginsberg with Gregory Corso and "Howl" with "Bomb." Nor can he bring himself to state that Ginsberg and Corso have published collections of poetry but only *"something called Howl,"* and *"something called Gasoline." The Naked Lunch,* he declares is "unintelligible to any soul who isn't on the stuff," (i.e. heroin.) And as for the author of *The Naked Lunch,* William Burroughs, he is *"terrified of almost everything, he never wanders far from the place and when he does go out, he hunches close to whatever buildings are along the way lizard-like for protection."* (*Lizard-like*, indeed!)

The hotel is, of course, a *"fleabag,"* a *"joint"* whose depraved, debauched and unhygienic inhabitants are *"living in a world of dreams induced by marijuana or heroin,"* and whose rooms are festooned with *"bras and blue jeans, panties and pajamas, all hanging from the ceiling like sausages from the rafters. Dirty dishes will be stacked in the sink that serves for everything – storage, stepladder and laundry bag."* Artist and author Brion Gysin's *"stuff"* (i.e. his painting and writing) amounts to no more than *"a gimmick,"* and the other writers and artists in the hotel are a pretentious and altogether *"pretty revolting"* lot. Resolutely lowbrow, the loutish author even flings a leering insult at author Mary McCarthy for presuming to champion Burroughs' novel. In sum, the article represents a not untypical instance of the ill-mannered and uninformed criticism often aimed at the Beats in the late 1950s and early 1960s. (*Sir*, vol. 21, no. 3, November 1964, pp. 22-25, 56.)

Two visitors to the hotel – the Scots poet Gael Turnbull and journalist and author Joseph Barry – have recorded their impressions in notes taken at the time. Turnbull's "Extracts from a Journal: Paris and Bill Burroughs, 1958," is centered upon his conversations with William Burroughs but he also describes an ascent to Gregory Corso's *"incredible sort of little attic room under the roof, to get to which one has almost to crawl on hands and feet around the last little spiral turn."* The walls of Corso's tiny room, he notes, are *"covered very beautifully with colored picture postcard prints, a bit like a stamp collection except that the result was more of a mosaic of Bagdad."* (*Mica*, 5, Winter 1962, pp. 6-11.) Barry's notes also present a description of Burroughs' room at the hotel: *"Walk up to fifth floor, room 30. Has two-burner gas stove on table in one corner. Washstand in other. Window looks across narrow street to chimney pots. Wardrobe with one other suit. Two chairs. Bed. Table with tired Spanish portable. ... Room warm. Not neat. Not disorderly. Just a room. Naked light bulb hanging over table. None over bed.*" (*The People of Paris,* Garden City: Doubleday, 1966, pp. 149-53.)

Set entirely in a room of the Beat Hotel, a short-story by Ann Morrissett titled "An Account of the Events Preceding the Death of Bill Burroughs" takes the form of a dialogue between a fist-person narrator and William S. Burroughs. (*Evergreen Review,* vol. 7, no. 29, March-April 1963, pp. 103-108.) The first-person narrator is, however, not a person, but a three foot alien disguised as a human woman, a serving officer in the Nova Police whose mission is to terminate William Burroughs for having discovered and revealed in his writing sensitive intelligence concerning the ongoing inter-galactic conflict between the Nova Mob and the Nova Police. (See The Nova Trilogy: *The Soft Machine, The Ticket that Exploded, Nova Express.*) The story which unfolds at "Nine Lies-the-Heart" accurately renders the spare furnishings of William Burroughs room: brown tea pot, radiator, typewriter, reel-to-reel tape recorder, the w.c. in the hall, Burroughs' collaboration with Mike Blake (another hotel resident) and correctly represents biographical details of Burroughs' life, mixing such realistic details with surreal invention. Ann Morrissett's "An Account" is an original and clever piece of fiction that in a witty and oblique fashion honors Burroughs' work. (In a letter to William Burroughs, Paul Bowles wrote that he had enjoyed reading the story. *In Touch: The Letters of Paul Bowles* New York: Farrar, Straus & Giroux, p. 350.)

Poetic paeans to no. 9 rue Gît-le.Coeur were composed by two hotel residents – Kay Johnson and Harold Norse. In her poem titled "...in Heaven at 9 Gît-le-Coeur" Kay Johnson celebrates the hotel and its guests as a kind of utopian enclave, a foretaste of paradise, and a model of what life on earth might be. (Curious, in light on her comments in Dixie Nimmo's *The Dream Palace* piece.) The population of the hotel comprehends "all languages ... all colors," living their individual lives side-by-side in human harmony. "Everyone" in the hotel, the poet declares, "has a dream / They talk from their souls / They listen to yours." Among the tolerant, forthright, creative hotel residents, there is room to unfold artistically and time, too, for fellowship. To be sure, the poet concedes, living conditions in the hotel are primitive: it is cold, the plumbing is rudimentary, often there is only bread to eat, nor are the residents immune to La Grippe, but the freedom, vitality and stimulation on offer and the sympathetic awareness prevalent among the hotel guests are worth whatever inconveniences are to be endured. In a world of convention and complacency, a world obsessed with material goods, power and status, the hotel at no. 9 rue Gît-le-Coeur represents for Kay Johnson, a haven, a "heaven," a kind of bohemian idyll or shabby urban *locus amoenus*. (*The Outsider*, vol. 1, no. 2, Summer 1962, pp. 31-33.)

At once a celebration of and lament for the demise of the Beat Hotel, Harold Norse's prose poem "The Death of 9, Rue Gît-le-Coeur," foregrounds the mysterious ambience of the old hotel. Norse records an incident when at three o'clock one afternoon a bat flew into his room through an open window and disappeared beneath a table while simultaneously a postcard of San Francisco's Chinatown dropped from the ceiling into the room. He also senses a strange significance in his having rented room no. 9 at no. 9 rue Gît-le-Coeur on the 9th day of the 9th month during the 9th year of his sojourn abroad. Like Kay Johnson, Norse savours life among

the kindred spirits who dwell in the hotel – the all-night jam
sessions with guitars and horns, the hashish visions, the
conversations and encounters – and extols the work that poets
and writers have accomplished while living there.

Norse grieves that the hotel has been sold to a hardnosed
businessman and his "hardfaced" wife who in order to attract a
more prosperous and respectable clientele are undertaking an
extensive remodelling the interior of the hotel. He expresses
annoyance with *Time* magazine for having referred to the hotel as
a "fleabag shrine," and declares that one day "the fleabag shrine
will be documented by art historians." Now in its sad last days,
even as Norse writes, the hotel was, he asserts, a "Dream Hotel,"
an interim conduit of a potent and mysterious energy. (*City Lights
Journal,* Number One, 1963, pp. 49-52.)

Scattered across the vast ocean of the internet are
personal memories of the Beat Hotel written by former residents.
In three short pieces "Adventures in the Beat Hotel" and "Tales
from the Beat Hotel," (both at http://www.litkicks.com) and "Eye
on the Beats," (http://www.geocities.com) Graham Seiden
recounts his experiences at no. 9 rue Gît-le-Coeur with Mack
Thomas, Gregory Corso, William Burroughs, Allen Ginsberg and
other hotel tenants: buying hashish, devising ways to pool the
hotel's scant electricity in order to operate a portable phonograph,
hatching schemes to make money, hanging out in cafés. Of
particular interest to me are the pragmatic details of Seiden's
three year sojourn at the hotel. His windowless room measured
approximately six by nine feet and cost twenty-one dollars per
month. The room was furnished only with an iron bed and a small
white porcelain washbasin. Seiden constructed shelves for his
books and bought a one-burner alcohol stove on which to prepare
meals. On cold mornings, to warm his room before getting out of

bed, he would spill a small pool of alcohol fuel on the bare tile floor and set it alight.

"Souvenirs of the Beat Hotel" by Baird Bryant (http://www.kerouacfest.com) is a first-person account of shooting up and scrying (using a bowl of water and the armoire mirror) with William Burroughs in his dim room at 9 rue Gît-le-Coeur, wacky Parisian sidewalk adventures with Gregory Corso, encountering Allen Ginsberg, much smoking of hashish, and scoring top-quality heroin for Mack Thomas (called Deke here.) It is also a chronicle of omens, visions, occult encounters, apparitions and visitations, culminating in a full-blown psychotic episode. There are in Bryant's piece few descriptive particulars but dramatic events are plentiful.

In a piece titled "The Humanity of the Machine: The Beat Hotel," (http://home.get2net.dk/abra-ken/humach.htm) and in "From Bellevue to Lynæs, "an interview with Lars Movin (http://www. Empty mirrorbooks.com/beat/kenneth-tindall.html) Ken Tindall recalls his life together with his Danish wife, Tove, in room 28 at 9 rue Gît-le-Coeur. Still vivid in his memory are the lukewarm water three times a week in the otherwise cold water faucets, the meagre and inadequate electricity, the resolute, all-embracing thrift of Madame Rachou, the amorous appeal among young women of Gregory Corso, learned latenight discussions of Wittgenstein among hotel residents, friendships with Jonathan Kozol and Piero Heliczer, conversations with William Burroughs and admiration of Burroughs' uncommon "battered leatherette" UHER reel-to-reel recording machine employed as a novel tool of literary composition, flogging copies of *The Paris Review* among café guests along the Boulevard Saint-Germain, and scoring hashish from the celebrated Hadj – esteemed purveyor of illegal drugs – at the Soleil du Maroc café on rue des Rosiers.

An amusing anecdote concerning a birthday party –
given for Tove – in Ken and Tove Tindall's outré room at the Beat
Hotel is related by Mel Birnkrant at his autobiographical website
"La Vie Parisienne 1958." (melbirnkrant.com) Birnkrant describes
the Tindall's room as having no light *other than a single candle,
inserted in a Chianti bottle that was covered in a multitude of
multicoloured drippings from the wax of countless candles,
collected over many years. The room was dominated by a massive
armoire, a kind of freestanding closet, nearly eight feet tall. Several
empty wine bottles stood on the top of it. Various objects were
placed here and there around the room, barely discernible in the dim
light. One aspect of their chamber was exceedingly strange. Tove
considered herself to be a painter. This was manifested by the fact
that she had carefully duplicated every shadow of every object in the
room, exactly as it was cast by the light of that single candle on the
wall behind it. Thus, all the objects and the candle were intended to
always remain in exactly the same place. If anything was moved,
Tove would quickly and carefully adjust it to make sure its real
shadow lined up perfectly with its matching painted shadow once
again."* In attendance at the party are Harold Chapman, Eunice
Richards, Mel Birnkrant and two black men: Ray and Bernard. Ray,
a dancer, is exceedingly drunk. After a joint is shared among the
guests, Ray insists on performing a dance, in preparation for
which he begins to remove his trousers. Losing his balance,
however, he falls against the armoire, overturning the bottles
perched atop it and knocking over the table with the single candle
upon it. The room is plunged into darkness and confusion. When
matches are lit to restore visibility, it is discovered that the wax-
covered Chianti bottle has been shattered on the tile floor. This
leaves a painted shadow on the floor without a bottle to be
projected onto it. *"Tove was inconsolable,"* Birnkrant writes.

A few last intriguing particulars and a suggestion for further study: Chester Himes thought that Madame Rachou "had obviously been the belle of her village." (*My Life of Absurdity: The Autobiography of Chester Himes,* vol. 2, New York: Doubleday, 1972, p. 75.) Pip Rau, also a Beat Hotel resident, has said that during the German Occupation of France, Madame Rachou was a member of the French Resistance, hiding in her hotel persons wanted for underground activities by the Gestapo or the French police. Her experience as a *résistante,* Pip Rau believes, inspired in Madame Rachou a form of cultural or social resistance during the postwar years, taking the form of a tolerant acceptance of and protectiveness toward her quirky, idiosyncratic, outsider, bohemian guests. (BBC broadcast by Andrew Hussey, *The Beat Hotel.)* The telephone number of the unnamed hotel at no. 9 rue Gît-le-Coeur was: ODEON 4166. (Letter from Weegee to Wilma Wilcox asking her to "Call Larry Yampolsky 9 rue Gît-le-Coeur ODEON 4166 room 37.") Madame Claude Odillard who took possession of the hotel in the 1980s and initiated its radical renovation recounts that while stripping the walls of the rooms down to their original medieval wooden beams, among the dusty ancient timbers thus exposed a 200 year-old bottle of wine was found. (Zahava Jones "Elegant Saint Germain des Prés" http://hotels.about.com/library/weekly/aa091798_1.htm) Adventures and misadventures with William Burroughs, Gregory Corso and others in the Beat Hotel are recounted in *Technicolor Dreamin'* a memoir by Karen Moller (who was a frequent visitor to though not a resident of the hotel.) Her highly readable book is published by Olympia Publishers: London, 2018.

Admirably memorialized in Harold Chapman's photos and Barry Miles' prose, the Beat Hotel has also been honoured in song, on film, with a BBC radio broadcast and on the internet.

Written and performed by Alan Taylor, a track titled "The Beat Hotel" (on CD *Hotels and Dreamers,* Stockfisch Records, SFR 357-60282) celebrates the Beat Hotel from its advent as a bohemian bastion in the 1950s to its closing in 1963. Mentioned by name in the text are Madame Rachou, William Burroughs, Allen Ginsberg, Gregory Corso and Alex Campbell. They and their fellow dwellers in the hotel – spaced out cosmonauts of inner space in hell-bent pursuit of *"Nirvana"* – are credited by Taylor with having *"opened up the road"* for a revolution in consciousness.

With ambient sounds from the streets of the Latin Quarter in Paris blended with the disembodied recorded voices of William Burroughs, Gregory Corso and Allen Ginsberg, together with interviews with former residents of no. 9 rue Gît-le-Coeur and others, an informed and evocative 30 minute sound-portrait of the Beat Hotel, assembled and narrated by Andrew Hussey (author and Professor of Cultural History at the School for Advanced Study, University of London) was broadcast on BBC Radio 4 Extra on 29 November 2017. Professor Hussey places the glory years of the Beat Hotel (1957-1963) in the context of the protracted Algerian War: the FLN bombings in Paris, the official curfews, the beatings by police, the killings and deportations of Algerian protestors. The turbulent, ominous yet curiously exciting atmosphere of the time – a country and a capital city in crisis, on edge – may in strange fashion, Hussey believes, have acted to energize certain of the radical artistic experiments essayed by occupants of the Beat Hotel. Former hotel resident Elliot Rudie recalls witnessing the brutal measures undertaken by the French police, hearing in the night streets of Paris the sound of automatic weapons, and being awakened in his room at the hotel by the concussion of bombs exploding nearby.

Hussey notes also the fertile intersection of key Beat Hotel habituées with figures in French literary culture (Louis Ferdinand Céline, Marcel Duchamp, Henri Michaux, Jean-Jacques Lebel, among others) and with North African culture (not least in the form of hashish, Moroccan trance music and Betty Bouthoul's book on Hassan-i-Sabba.) The Professor further argues that the artistic activities and social attitudes of Beat Hotel occupants represented at the time "the red-hot center of the avant-garde" in Anglo-American culture, and that this fleeting, free-wheeling "bohemian utopia," this mutually inspiring collective experiment "blew the lid off" an older, more staid culture. Here was where "the future was being dreamt up," he contends: "so much that happened in the Beat Hotel prophesied the 21st century."

Oliver Harris, author and Professor of American Literature at Keele University – in conversation with the narrator of the broadcast – expresses his belief that the Beat Hotel was a vortical locus of inspiration and innovation: "a unique phenomenon. I don't think it could have happened just anywhere else at any other time." In separate interviews, former Beat Hotel residents Pip Rau, Harold Chapman and Elliot Rudie all concur that there was about the hotel a special spirit, an atmosphere and an energy that were truly magical.

In cyberspace there exists a virtual establishment calling itself "Beat Hotel," (to be found at beathotel.co.uk and at beathotelshow.tumblr.com) the purpose of which, a mission statement announces, is to provide a place *"that combines the best of film, literature, art and music. It resonates with the old ethos of the Beat Generation ... It is a home for freaks and artists out there who are looking for somewhere they can speak their minds and share ideas."* The site also advertises and seeks funding for *"The*

Beat Hotel: An adult comedy puppet show inspired by the coolest hotel this side of bohemia."

A documentary history of the glory days of no. 9 rue Gît-le-Coeur, an 82 minute film titled *The Beat Hotel* (2012) strives to render the ambience and experience of the nameless ramshackle hotel and its lively bohemian residents by means of a fast-moving jazzy blend of interviews with literary scholars and former hotel residents, dramatic re-enactments of incidents, readings from key Beat texts written at the hotel, film clips from the streets of Paris, photographs, drawings, special effects and animated sequences. There are interviews with and commentaries by erstwhile hotel-dwellers Harold Chapman, Elliot Rudie, Cyclops Lester and Peter Golding. Sage beat scholars Regina Weinreich, Oliver Harris and Barry Miles suggest cultural contexts, and oldtime beat-friendly hotel visitors Jean-Jacques Lebel and Jürgen Ploog pitch in with reminiscences and anecdotes. Madame Claude Odillard also makes an appearance, as does too, an ancient George Whitman of the nearby Shakespeare & Co. bookshop. And by way of surreal incongruity, there are views of the present exterior and interior of the elaborately adorned, transmogrified hotel.

Among the film's various participants there is agreement that the Beat Hotel was a very special and significant site. It was, owing to Madame Rachou, "a zone of tolerance," and owing to the diverse, unconventional, creatively-inclined hotel residents, "bohemia working at its best." The "insurrection of the mind" fomented in its dim-lit, cold-water rooms helped to shape many important cultural impulses that were to animate the decades that followed. (*The Beat Hotel* directed by Alan Govenar. Drawings by Elliot Rudie. Photographs by Harold Chapman. Animations by Alan Hatchett and Blas Garcia. Produced by Documentary Arts.)

After Madame Rachou turned the key one final time in the door of the nameless old hotel at number 9 rue Gît-le-Coeur, the interior was renovated and remodelled under the direction of the new owners, Monsieur and Madame Laigle. The fabled, rundown, disreputable establishment was reborn as a two-star hotel named Au Vieux Paris. Although much transformed, this new incarnation of the hotel was far from luxurious. There were no telephones, televisions, radios, minibars, hairdryers or other amenities in the rooms. The walls of the rooms were covered in yellow, orange and brown floral wallpaper and were furnished with a radiator, a modern brown varnished wardrobe, a washbasin, and new beds with headboards and reading lamps. Across the width of the bed lay the traditional French *traversin,* or bolster pillow, a firm, tubular sausage-shaped pillow. The ancient winding stairway was still the only way to ascend from the lobby to the rooms and toilets were still located in the stairwell, though the "Turkish" squat toilets were now replaced by standard "sit down" white porcelain toilets. Located in a room behind the registration desk in the lobby was a breakfast room for hotel guests. Breakfast consisted of a baguette with butter and jam, a small ceramic pitcher of dark, rich coffee and a small ceramic pitcher of thick, warm milk. In the lobby, between the registration desk and the doors stood a television set which could be watched in the evening (French channels only, of course) from a small sofa and two stuffed chairs. Through the 1980s, the upper stories of the hotel remained untouched, unremodelled. In these empty, ghostly corridors the knobless old doors of the now silent rooms with their stencilled room numbers still visible were firmly locked.

The hotel Au Vieux Paris was subsequently purchased by Madame Claude Odillard who beginning in 1991 undertook further and far more extensive remodelling of the interior, converting the premises into a Four Star hotel, now renamed the Relais Hotel du Vieux Paris. The current hotel features air conditioning, spacious rooms with exposed beams and wall fabrics by designer Pierre Frey, futon chairs, private marble bathrooms with hairdryers and showers with water massage jets (and in the suites, jacuzzis), minibars, color televisions with numerous channels, wifi, direct dial telephones and wall safes in each room. The hotel describes itself as being both "business-friendly" and "family friendly."

In the late winter of 1996, for the first time in 34 years, Allen Ginsberg crossed the threshold of no. 9 rue Gît-le-Coeur and entered the lobby of the old hotel, which had in the interim – as described above – been utterly transformed. With the owner's permission and accompanied by free-lance journalist, Peter Mikelbank, Ginsberg roamed freely about the premises, mounting the winding stairway to the location of his former room. In wonder and dismay, with fascination and horror, he examined the now elegant rooms and well kept corridors once so familiar to him, now so thoroughly remodelled and reconfigured as to be unrecognizable. Sighing, Ginsberg remarked to Mikelbank: "It's all changed." Then, quoting W.B. Yeats, he added: "All changed. Changed utterly. A terrible beauty is born." ("Easter, 1916".) Inquiring what the price of a night's lodging at the hotel was at present, Ginsberg was told that it was 1000 francs a night or the equivalent of $175. Shaking his head in sad amusement, Ginsberg said "I don't think we paid that for a year's rent." ("Allen Ginsberg Returns to the Beat Hotel and It Isn't the Same" *The San Francisco Examiner* March 17, 1996.)

On the first of July in 2009, a glass plaque commemorating the Beat Hotel was placed on the façade of the Relais Hotel de Vieux Paris. The text on the plaque is in French, reading in

English translation: "Here lived: B. Gysin, H. Norse, G. Corso, A. Ginsberg, P. Orlovsky, I. Sommerville. Here W. Burroughs finished *Naked Lunch* (1959.)"

Reverberations roll on and on. At Desert Hot Springs in California there is a hotel calling itself *The Beat Hotel*. The hotel consists of eight suites, each containing a sleeping room, a small kitchen, a desk and a manual typewriter. The hotel contains original art, manuscripts, books, photographs and other materials intended "to evoke the presence" of William Burroughs and the Beat Generation. (Steven Lowe at www.palmspringslife.com). In the United Kingdom, the annual Glastonbury Festival of music and the performing arts has since 2011 featured a bar and venue "sort of inspired by the Beat Generation" called *The Beat Hotel*. Recently, *The Beat Hotel* relocated to Marrakech, Morocco, assuming the role there of an annual festival of live music, DJs "and a talks programme with some of today's great minds and voices." (beathotel.benkitching.uk) In Bangkok, Thailand there is also a (3 star) *Beat Hotel* that attempts to emulate the original Beat Hotel in having illustrations and graffiti on the bare white walls of the rooms.

In January of 1997, an exhibit titled "Sinclair Beiles and the Beat Hotel," sponsored by The British Council and the Institut Francais d'Afrique du Sud, was held in Carfax, Johannesburg, South Africa. The exhibition featured a reconstruction of the façade of the hotel at 9 rue Gît-le-Coeur as it appeared in the 1950s, as well as reconstructions of two of the rooms. Based on photographs of the hotel taken by Harold Chapman, the reconstituted Beat Hotel was designed by James de Villiers and featured duplicates of numerous (now historical) items such as sinks, pots and pans, lamps, bottles, tables, an exact replica of one of the beds, and reproductions of Beat Hotel paintings and graffiti.

I have in these notes scrupulously avoided setting forth any information appearing elsewhere. The achievements of the most celebrated former residents of the Beat Hotel, William Burroughs, Brion Gysin, Ian Sommerville and Gregory Corso are well-known and have been admirably treated by Barry Miles and others. In the following – with the aim of suggesting something of the range of talent and intelligence once gathered within the ancient walls of the Beat Hotel – I would like to furnish brief accounts of the careers and accomplishments of some of the lesser known alumni of number 9 rue Gît-le-Coeur. (Some former residents I found to be untraceable.)

Guy Harloff (1933-1991) exhibited his paintings in venues worldwide and has work included in the permanent collection The National Gallery of Art and elsewhere. He was the author of *Unself Portrait* (1989) and is the subject of *Guy Harloff: L'olandese volante* by Colombo Nicoletta (2016.) **Robert Grosvenor**'s sculptures and photographs are held in the collections of the Museum of Modern Art N.Y., the Hirshhorn Museum, the Walker Art Center, the Museum of Contemporary Art L.A., the Whitney Museum of American Art and elsewhere. *Patrick Shelley* (1928-2012) is the subject of a monograph titled *Des Yeux Pour Voir* by Jean Bothorel (1996.) A retrospective of his artwork was held at the Galerie d'art ô Marches du Palais, and his paintings are part of the permanent collection of the Musée Paul Valéry. **Herbert Kohl** is the celebrated author of more than forty books, including *36 Children* (1967) and *I Won't Learn from You* (1995.) **Kenneth Tindall** has published two novels: *Great Heads* (1969) and *The Banks of the Sea* (1987.)

Mack Sheldon Thomas (1928-2016) published two novels – *Gumbo* (1965) and *The Total Beast* (1970) – and wrote jazz criticism for *Kulchur* magazine. He is the subject of a biography by

Jim Welton titled *Mack Thomas: The Total Beat* (2016.) **Bob Thompson** (1937-1966) despite an untimely death achieved the reputation and status of an important figure in African-American art. His work is to be found in the Smithsonian American Art Museum, the Museum of Contemporary Art L.A. and elsewhere. The Whitney Museum mounted a retrospective of his work in 1988. **Thomas Neurath** served as Managing Director of Thames & Hudson Ltd. and is currently chairman of that esteemed publishing organization. **Stan Persky** is the author of many books including *Wrestling the Angel* (1977) *Autobiography of a Tattoo* (1997) and *Letter from Berlin* (2017.) He teaches philosophy at Capilano University in North Vancouver.

Alan Eager (1927-2003) following his Beat Hotel days, played tenor saxophone with Charles Mingus, Dizzy Gillespie, Chet Baker and Frank Zappa. He also pursued competitive auto racing. **John Howley**'s paintings have been exhibited in Germany, England, Israel and Australia. He also plays piano with a jazz trio. **Harold Chapman**'s photographs are collected in *Vanishing France* (1975), *Everyman's France* (1982) and *The Beat Hotel* (1984.) Together with William Sansom, he assembled *Victorian Life in Photographs* (1974.) Chapman is the subject of an article by Ian McEwan entitled "A Spy in the Name of Art," published in the *Saturday Review* of *The Guardian*. **Gottfried John** is an actor whose stage successes roles in contemporary and classic drama. He appeared in a number of films directed by Rainer Werner Fassbinder, various American and British tv series, and portrayed the Russian villain, General Ourumov, in the James Bond film, *The Golden Eye* (1995.)

Vertamae Kali Smart-Grosvenor (1937-2016) became a culinary anthropologist, a food writer, a performer, a broadcaster and the author of: *Vibration Cooking, or the Travel Notes of a*

Geechee Girl (1970), *Thursday and Every Other Sunday Off* (1972), *Black Atlantic Cooking* (1990), *Vertamae Cooks in America's Family Kitchen* (1996) and *Vertamae Cooks Again* (1999.) **Peter Golding** is a fashion designer and musician. He created the first designer jean in 1970 and the first stretch denim jean in 1978. He opened a clothing store, ACE, on King's Road in Chelsea, and in recognition of his contribution to British design was invited by the Queen to Buckingham Palace. **Robin Page** (1932-2015) exhibited his sculptures, paintings and prints internationally, and was a participant in the Fluxus movement. **Anthony Benjamin** (1931-2002) painter, sculptor, printmaker, had one-man exhibitions in the U.K, Australia, the U.S.A., Norway, Sweden, Belgium and Denmark, and taught art at colleges in Canada, the U.S.A. and the U.K.

 Alex Campbell (1931-1987) played folk clubs in the United Kingdom and throughout Europe. He recorded extensively. **Pip Rau** runs a shop, Rau Gallery, London, selling dresses, waist-coats, robes and cloth from Central Asia and the Middle East. **Stella Tohl** (1933-2010) lived in Santa Fe, New Mexico, where she was a dedicated community health educator and social worker. **Angus MacLise** (1938-1979) was a writer, musician, composer, painter, calligrapher and first drummer of *The Velvet Underground*. His many books include: *Dream Weapon* (1970), *The Cloud Doctrine* (1974) and *The Map of Dusk* (1984.) A major retrospective titled "Dreamweapon: The Art and Life of Angus MacLise" was held at the Steohen Kasher Gallery N.Y.C. in 2011. **Olivia de Hauelleville** is the author of *Maria* (Paris: 1958) and *Pilgrimage to Java* (2000.) She was for a time a columnist for the *International Times* (London.)

 Jonathan Kozol published a novel *The Fume of Poppies* in 1958, and went on to become a distinguished writer of nonfiction and a social activist whose many works include: *Death at an Early Age* (1967), *Savage Inequalities* (1992) and *The Shame of the Nation* (2000.) **Michael Gothard** (1939-1992) acted in a number of television series and several films, including *The Three Musketeers, The Four Musketeers* and Ken Russell's *The Devils.* He played the villain Emile Leopold Locque in the 1981 James Bond film, *For Your Eyes Only.* **Elliot Rudie** served as Community Artist and Art Teacher at Bettyhill in Sutherland, Scotland, Principal Teacher of Art at Farr High School, and Visual Arts Co-ordinator for the Northlands Festival (1993-2001.) A retrospective exhibition of his artwork was held at the Thurso Art Gallery in 2019. **Derek Raymond** penname of **Robert Cook** (1931-1994) was considered the father of British *noir.* He authored numerous crime novels, including *The Crust on its Uppers* (1962) and *He Died with His Eyes Open* (1984) together with a literary memoir titled *The Hidden Files* (1992.)

Keith Lorenz worked for many years as a correspondent in Southeast Asia. He is the author of *Paul Chesley: A Photographic Voyage* (2013), "Singapore and its Neighbors" in *East-West Perspectives* (Summer 1982), is a contributor to other publications, and founder and president of Bamboo Republic (Asian cuisine?) **Kay Johnson** authored *Human Songs* (a collection of poems) published by San Franciso publisher City Lights in 1964. Her essay "Proximity" appeared in *Journal for the Protection of All Beings* (City Lights: S.F. 1961.) Her mysterious life is the subject of "Poet Kay Johnson, aka Kaya" by David Gitin and various contributors at emptymirrorbooks.com/beat/kaja. Her essay "Proximity" was reprinted by The Sun Magazine and is available at thesunmagazine.org/issues/109/proximity.

During the 1970s and 1980s, on four occasions, my wife and I stayed at the two-star hotel Au Vieux Paris. Once a young desk clerk permitted me to descend through a wooden trap door located behind the registration desk into the medieval vaulted cellar beneath the hotel. Alas, I could find there no trace of the past, only stacks of dusty plastic chairs with steel legs. On another occasion, I mounted the winding wooden stairway all the way up to the two topmost garret rooms: nos. 40 and 41. (I have mentioned previously that the top stories of the hotel had not at this time been remodelled. They remained as they had been during the Beat era apart from the fact that all the doors to the numbered rooms were locked.) The door to room no. 41, where Gregory Corso once invoked his muse and engineered his "Bomb," was firmly sealed, but the door to no. 40 (top right of the stairs) was ajar. The room was accessible. Except for the removal of the bed which must once have been the tiny room's only permanent furnishing, the room itself appeared not to have been altered since the closure of the hotel in 1963. The venerable hexagonal red ceramic tiles were still on the floor. A small soot-covered porcelain washbasin remained attached to one wall. (Powdery grains of soot having entered the chamber through thin gaps in the loose-fitting skylight.) Apparently the little room was used by the hotel for storage, crowded with broken chairs, broken light fixtures, metal bed frames, colored plastic buckets draped with rags, a stringy floor mop, and other clutter.

On one wall, however, hanging askew, attached from one corner by a single thumb tack (where originally each corner had been pinned to the wall) hung a sheet of paper, blackened with a fine dust. Upon examining it and perceiving that it was a painting, I removed it from the wall. The area on the wall immediately behind the painting (protected by it from exposure to sunlight) was clearly of a far lighter color than the rest of the wall, both where the painting had dangled and where it had originally hung suspended by both thumb tacks. Plainly, the paper had been pinned (then half-pinned) there for a long time. With never a pang of conscience I assumed possession of this intriguing object, triumphantly transporting it downstairs to my room where using soft tissue I carefully cleared from its surface the grime of decades. Rendered in five now faded colors, the painting represented in stylized fashion a charging brown bull assailing and overturning a brightly clad matador whose limbs splay and sprawl to all sides as the force of the bull's impact causes his body to fly head over heels into the air. The thick textured paper – originally white, as evidenced by the small circular surface in the upper right hand of the painting which had long been covered by the single steadfast thumbtack – was not yellow but *brown* with age. (See Appendix II, page 47 for color-enhanced reproduction.) The apparent age of the painting, the depth of the grime adhering to its surface, the markedly contrasting lighter coloring of the wall just behind the painting, and its inconspicuous, unregarded placement on the wall of an unremodelled garret storage room persuaded me that in all likelihood it had been left hanging there – overlooked or abandoned as something of little worth – by the last occupant of that room.

This curious artefact – derelict relic of a former era – might be seen to serve as an emblem of the spirit that animated the Beat Hotel. The painting depicts an unexpected reversal, an overturning of the programmed course of events. According to long-established practice, it is the matador who controls the performance in the bull ring, deceiving and maneuvering the bull. But in this instance, the bull will not be subdued. The bull refuses, as it were, to play the game on the matador's terms and, instead, upends him, overthrowing the artificial control he exercises. In a similar manner, many of the ideas and attitudes fostered in the

Beat Hotel, and much of the artistic and conceptual innovation undertaken there had as a common denominator an oppositional, adversarial character, a shared quality of resistance to convention and custom, a refusal to comply with constrictive categories, artificial restraints and external control.

The nameless old hotel on an ancient street in Paris – enduring there in quiet obscurity through the years and wars – served for a season both as a last bastion of the radical explorations and experiments of a late Modernist sensibility ("making it new:" new visions, new forms) and as an outstation of a larger, older, persistent, ever-unfolding enterprise long spearheaded by poets, painters and others to extend literary and artistic representation, and to help reshape or redeem human perception. A fleabag no more, no. 9 rue Gît-le-Coeur has, indeed, become a shrine.

Appendix I

RÉPUBLIQUE FRANÇAISE
POSTES
5c
HOTEL
85 — PARIS — Inondations de janvier 1910 — La rue Git-le-Cœur   G. M.

Appendix II

www.ingramcontent.com/pod-product-compliance
Lightning Source LLC
Chambersburg PA
CBHW071252130726
47998CB00003B/1164